SCHOLASTIC

Reading Passages That Build Comprehension

CONTEXT CLUES

BY LINDA WARD BEECH

NEW YORK • TORONTO • LONDON • AUCKLAND • SYDNEY
MEXICO CITY • NEW DELHI • HONG KONG • BUENOS AIRES

Teaching *Resources*

Contents

Cover design by Maria Lilja
Interior design by Holly Grundon
Interior art by Mike Gordon

ISBN 0-439-55426-8
Copyright © 2005 by Linda Ward Beech.
All rights reserved.
Printed in the U.S.A.

8 9 10   40   14 13 12 11 10

Introduction

Reading comprehension involves numerous thinking skills. Using context clues to understand word meaning is one such skill. A reader who is adept at using context clues makes better sense of a text and reads more smoothly and efficiently. This book will help you help students learn to recognize context clues to decipher word meaning and to build vocabulary. Use the pages that follow to teach this skill to students and to give them practice in employing it.

Using This Book

Pages 5-7

After introducing context clues to students (see page 4), duplicate and pass out pages 5–7. Use page 5 to help students review and practice what they have just learned about using context clues. By explaining their thinking, students are using metacognition to analyze how they recognized and utilized these clues. Pages 6–7 give students a model of the practice pages to come. They also provide a model of the thinking students might use in choosing the best word or words to approximate the meaning of an unknown word.

Page 8

Use this page as a pre-assessment to find out how students think when they use context clues. When going over these pages with students, discuss how different clues help them understand the meaning of an unfamiliar word.

Pages 9-43

These pages offer practice in using context clues. After reading each paragraph, students should fill in the bubble in front of the correct answer for each question.

Suggest that students substitute their answer choice for the boldfaced word in a passage. If they have selected the correct answer, the word or words should make sense in the sentence.

Pages 44-46

After they have completed the practice pages, use these pages to assess the way students think when they use context clues.

Page 47

You may wish to keep a record of students' progress as they complete the practice pages. Sample comments that will help you guide students toward improving their skills might include:

- reads carelessly
- misunderstands text
- fails to recognize context clues
- doesn't apply prior knowledge
- doesn't focus on the logic or sense of the text

Teacher Tip

For students who need extra help, you might suggest that they keep pages 5–7 with them to use as examples when they complete the practice pages.

Mini-Lesson: Teaching About Context Clues

1. Introduce the concept: Write this sentence on the chalkboard:

That package is too _____ for Jenny to carry.

Invite students to supply a word for the blank in the sentence.

2. Model thinking: After students have suggested words such as *heavy* or *big* for the sentence, help them explore why they chose these words by modeling how they might think aloud.

A package that is heavy or big is usually hard to carry. These words make sense in the sentence.

3. Define the skill: Point out that in determining an appropriate word to use in the blank, students looked at the other words in the sentence. Explain that this is what is meant by **context**. The words *too* and *carry* are good clues that the missing word might be *heavy*. The word *package* also provides important information.

Explain that when students read a passage and come to an unfamiliar word, they can use context clues to try to figure out the word's meaning. Explain that these clues can be in the same sentence or in other sentences in the passage. Share these examples of context clues with students:

- The meaning is clearly given.
  *The goats lived at the **timberline**. A timberline is where trees stop growing on a mountainside.*

- An example is given.
  *Many animals **migrate** to warmer places each autumn. For example, some hummingbirds fly to Mexico.*

- The meaning is restated.
  *The monkey **outwitted**, or <u>outsmarted</u>, the keeper.*

- Other words help describe a word.
  *The **lame** elk was <u>injured</u> and <u>limping</u>.*

- The word has a known prefix or suffix.
  *The team was **unhappy** about its loss.*

4. Practice the skill: Use Practice Pages 9–43 to give students practice in comparing and contrasting.

Name_____ Date_____

What Is Context?

You read a paragraph. Suddenly, you come to a word you don't know. What does a reader do? A good reader might try to figure out the word meaning by using context. A reader might think:

What other words in the sentence and paragraph suggest possible meanings?

How is this word used in the sentence (or paragraph)?

What clues can I find?

These questions help a reader use **context**. Context is the setting in which a word appears. The context for a word can be a sentence or a paragraph. It can also be a longer passage.

Read the paragraph below, and then complete each sentence.

Our Solar System

We live in a **solar** system. The most important part of this system is the sun. In fact, the solar system could be called the "sun system." The nine planets in our solar system all move around the sun.

1. The word **solar** must have something to do with the

   _____

   _____.

2. One context clue is

   _____

   _____.

3. Another context clue is

   _____

   _____.

4. I can check my idea about the word by

   _____

   _____.

Name _____ Date _____

Using Context Clues

Study these two pages. They show how a student used context clues to figure out word meanings.

Read the paragraph. Then fill in the bubble that best completes the sentence.

Abe's Clothes

When Abe Lincoln was a boy, he wore clothes that were made at home. His woolen socks were knitted by hand. Even the cloth for his shirts was woven at home. Abe's **breeches** were made of deerskin. However, it was not good to wear these breeches in the rain. If they got wet, they shrank. Abe had a mark on each leg from breeches that got too tight in the rain!

In this paragraph, the word *breeches* must mean

○ A. towels

Towels are not clothing. This paragraph is about clothing. Also, towels are not made of leather or deerskin.

○ C. bearskin

The paragraph says breeches were made of deerskin. I don't think bearskin makes sense here.

● B. pants

Breeches could be pants. Tight pants could leave a mark on your leg.

I am going to fill in **B.** This word makes the most sense. The context clues suggest that breeches are pants.

Using Context Clues

Read the paragraph. Then fill in the
bubble that best completes the sentence.

A Solemn Day

Drums rolled as the band went by. The crowd watched quietly. A few people were crying. Many wore black. Then it was time for the mayor to speak. He made a **solemn** speech. In it he told how much the great judge would be missed. People bowed their heads at the end of this serious speech.

In this paragraph, the word *solemn* must mean

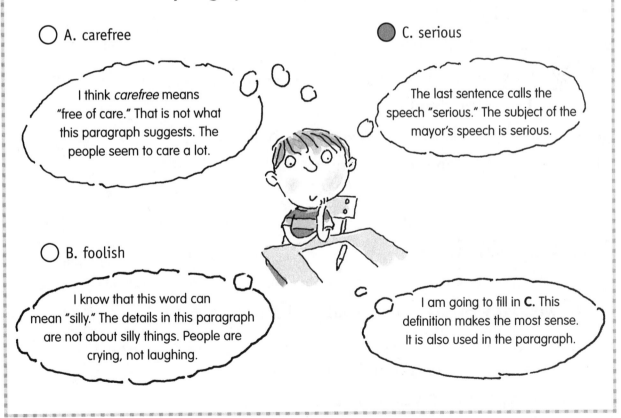

A. carefree

I think *carefree* means "free of care." That is not what this paragraph suggests. The people seem to care a lot.

C. serious

The last sentence calls the speech "serious." The subject of the mayor's speech is serious.

B. foolish

I know that this word can mean "silly." The details in this paragraph are not about silly things. People are crying, not laughing.

I am going to fill in **C.** This definition makes the most sense. It is also used in the paragraph.

Name_____ Date_____

Thinking About Information

Read each paragraph. Then fill in the bubble that best completes each sentence. Underline the parts of the paragraph that helped you.

Maine Names

The state of Maine has a very long _____. Many of its towns are on the sea. Some of these are named for water animals. For example, one town is called Cape Porpoise. Two others are Seal Harbor and Swans Island.

1. The best word for the blank is
   ○ A. name
   ○ B. coast
   ○ C. ocean

Mushrooms

Most plants make their own food in order to live. Mushrooms do not. Mushrooms _____ by getting food from their surroundings. For example, a mushroom living on dead wood gets food material from that.

2. The best word for the blank is
   ○ A. survive
   ○ B. smell
   ○ C. poison

A Windy Walk

Mr. Wilcox went out for his afternoon walk. It was later than usual. A sharp wind blew up and made him _____. Mr. Wilcox zipped up his jacket and put his hands in his pockets. Autumn was coming.

3. The best word for the blank is
   ○ A. laugh
   ○ B. fall
   ○ C. shiver

Practice Page 1

Name_____ Date_____

Read each paragraph. Then fill in the bubble
that best completes each sentence.

Using Plants

Long ago, people used plants to make colorful **dyes**. They boiled plants in water. Different plants gave off different colors. For example, boiled acorns made a light brown, and beets made a bright pink. The skins from certain onions made an orange-colored dye. Once the dyes were ready, people dipped wool or other cloth into them.

1. In this paragraph, the word **dyes** must mean
   ○ A. flags
   ○ B. colorings
   ○ C. foods

The Singing Bird

From her window, Mindy could see an old apple tree. Each morning a bird sang to her from a **bough** of the tree. Then the bird would hop to another branch and sing some more. Mindy was always sorry when she had to leave for school.

2. In this paragraph, the word **bough** must mean
   ○ A. branch
   ○ B. song
   ○ C. trunk

Practice Page 2

Name_____ Date_____

Read each paragraph. Then fill in the bubble that best completes each sentence.

Gilbert Stuart

Gilbert Stuart was an artist. He lived during the early years of our country. Stuart often painted pictures of the famous people of his time. Perhaps his most famous **portrait** is of George Washington. Many copies have been made of this painting. Stuart also painted other American leaders, such as John Adams and James Madison.

1. In this paragraph, the word **portrait** must mean
   ○ A. a popular landscape
   ○ B. past national leader
   ○ C. picture of a person

Puppy Trouble

Buster is Dee's new puppy. He is also Dee's new problem. Buster is very loving, but he isn't so good at learning. When Dee calls the puppy, Buster comes **bounding** over the gate and through Dad's garden. Dirt flies and plants get crushed. "He's not supposed to jump over the fence!" yells Dad. Dee is thinking about taking Buster to dog school.

2. In this paragraph, the word **bounding** must mean
   ○ A. walking
   ○ B. leaping
   ○ C. crawling

Practice Page **3** Name_____ Date_____

Read each paragraph. Then fill in the bubble that best completes each sentence.

What a Lizard!

Have you ever seen a chuckwalla? This animal is a kind of lizard. The chuckwalla lives in deserts. In the spring and early summer, it eats desert flowers. If anything **alarms** the chuckwalla, it hides in between rocks. The frightened lizard pumps itself up with air. That way it cannot be pulled from its hiding place. When not eating or hiding, the chuckwalla sleeps up to seven months a year!

1. In this paragraph, the word **alarms** must mean

○ A. scares

○ B. catches

○ C. pulls

The Eyeglasses

Bev was upset. The eye doctor said she needed to wear glasses. Bev had a big **scowl** on her face as she tried them on. She wouldn't even look in the mirror. Nothing her mother said made Bev feel better. Then her friend Joe came over. "Hey, cool glasses," he said. "I want frames just like yours." Bev's scowl turned into a smile.

2. In this paragraph, the word **scowl** must mean

○ A. grin

○ B. stare

○ C. frown

Practice Page 4

Name_____ Date_____

Read each paragraph. Then fill in the bubble
that best completes each sentence.

Going West

In the 1840s thousands of people traveled to the West. Many of these travelers followed the Oregon Trail. This **route** stretched from Independence, Missouri, to Oregon. It led over mountains and rivers. It crossed miles of flatland, too. Most families traveled along the route in wagons. It was a long and hard trip.

1. In this paragraph, the word **route** must mean
   ○ A. grin
   ○ B. part of a plant
   ○ C. path or trail

To the Playground

Peter did not want to go to the playground. Tom did. Peter was older, and Tom couldn't go without him. So Tom began to **coax** his brother. He talked about how much fun they would have. He offered to share his toys. He promised to let Peter have his pie at dinner. Finally, Peter gave in. The two boys went off to the playground.

2. In this paragraph, the word **coax** must mean
   ○ A. make someone unhappy
   ○ B. get mad and hurt someone
   ○ C. get someone to do something

Practice Page 5

Name_____ Date_____

Read each paragraph. Then fill in the bubble
that best completes each sentence.

A Great Grass

Bamboo is a type of grass. But unlike other grasses,
bamboo has a woody **stalk**. This giant grass can grow
up to 70 feet tall. People make many things from the bamboo
stem. These include fishing rods, birdcages, and furniture. In
some countries, people
live in bamboo houses.
It's no wonder that
bamboo is called
a treasure in
many parts of
the world.

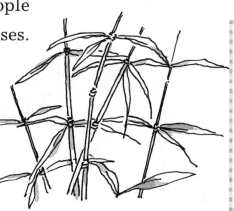

1. In this paragraph, the
   word **stalk** must mean
   ○ A. stem
   ○ B. flower
   ○ C. seed

Where's Bootsy?

When Fran came home, her cat wasn't
there to greet her. Fran looked in
the kitchen. She checked the other rooms
too. "Here, kitty, kitty," she called. Fran
began to worry. Her voice rose to a **holler**.
"Bootsy! Where are you?" Then Fran heard
a noise. It came from a closet. Bootsy was
locked in by mistake.

2. In this paragraph, the
   word **holler** must mean
   ○ A. hollow
   ○ B. shout
   ○ C. whisper

Practice Page 6

Name_____ Date_____

Read each paragraph. Then fill in the bubble
that best completes each sentence.

Cook's Trip

In 1770 Captain James Cook was sailing in the Pacific Ocean. He was on his way home to England. A bad storm came up. Cook's ship was blown toward some land. He sailed along the shore. On the land he saw many new plants and animals. Captain Cook decided to **claim** the land for England. The land was known as Australia. England ruled it for many years.

1. In this paragraph, the word **claim** must mean
   ○ A. make a map of
   ○ B. make a sudden sound
   ○ C. state the right to own

Bret and Brad

The twins were alike in many ways. But when it came to swimming, they had different ideas. Bret liked to get into the water slowly. Sometimes he took quite a long time. But Brad liked to get in fast. He would **plunge** right in and come up laughing. Bret could never understand this.

2. In this paragraph, the word **plunge** must mean
   ○ A. play fairly
   ○ B. enter quickly
   ○ C. throw down

Practice Page 7

Name_____ Date_____

Read each paragraph. Then fill in the bubble
that best completes each sentence.

The Story of Rudolph

Have you heard of Rudolph the Red-Nosed Reindeer? Rudolph first appeared in a poem in 1939. Copies of the poem were given to children by a store in Chicago. Rudolph became very popular. In 1949 a **composer** named Johnny Marks wrote a song about the shiny-nosed reindeer. Today his song about Rudolph is still a holiday favorite.

1. In this paragraph, the word **composer** must mean
   - ○ A. someone who writes poetry
   - ○ B. someone who writes music
   - ○ C. someone who works in a store

☆ ☆ ☆

Rob's Job

The Dells had a big fireplace. On snowy winter days they often lit a fire. Rob's job was to make sure there was plenty of wood to burn. He would take his sled to the woodshed. There he loaded logs onto the sled. Then he would **haul** the wood back to the house and bring it in to burn.

2. In this paragraph, the word **haul** must mean
   - ○ A. chop
   - ○ B. pull
   - ○ C. burn

Practice Page 8

Name_____ Date_____

Read each paragraph. Then fill in the bubble
that best completes each sentence.

In the U.S.

Parts of the United States are
rolling meadows called **prairies**.
These regions have deep, rich soil.
The land is mostly flat. Prairies do not
get enough rain for many trees to grow.
But grasses grow well on them. These
areas are good for growing grains such
as wheat and oats. The prairies are also
good for raising animals that eat grass,
such as cattle.

1. In this paragraph, the word
   prairies must mean
   ○ A. drylands
   ○ B. wetlands
   ○ C. grasslands

Abby's Talk

Abby was asked to give a talk
in school. She was **eager** to
do this. Abby liked to talk. She was
good at getting people to listen. She
could make people laugh, too. When
the time for her talk came, Abby
was ready. She gave a great talk.

2. In this paragraph, the word **eager**
   must mean
   ○ A. wanting to do something
   ○ B. unhappy about being chosen
   ○ C. not interested in a project

Practice Page 9

Name_____   Date_____

Read each paragraph. Then fill in the bubble
that best completes each sentence.

The Ocean Floor

Most people think of the bottom of the ocean as a flat place. But it is not. It is much like the rest of Earth—uneven. In some places the ocean bottom slopes downward from the shore. In other places it is flat. There are also lots of mountains. Between the mountains are deep **trenches**. The Mariana Trench in the Pacific Ocean is almost 40,000 feet deep.

1. In this paragraph, the word **trenches** must mean
   ○ A. big ditches
   ○ B. areas where the land trembles
   ○ C. mountains on the floor of the ocean

Fred the Fish

Fred was a very smart fish. He lived in a peaceful river. Nothing much happened there unless people came around. Then Fred had to be **alert**. A yummy worm might mean a trap. If Fred wasn't careful, he could end up as someone's supper. He had seen it happen to many careless fish.

2. In this paragraph, the word **alert** must mean
   ○ A. watchful
   ○ B. careless
   ○ C. sleepy

Practice Page 10

Name_____ Date_____

Read each paragraph. Then fill in the bubble
that best completes each sentence.

Languages of the World

Not everyone in the world speaks English. In fact, more people speak Chinese than any other language in the world. English is the second-most-spoken language. Other **major** languages are Russian and Hindi. More than 300 million people speak Hindi. Most of these people are from India.

1. In this paragraph, the word **major** must mean
   ○ A. foreign and unknown
   ○ B. large and important
   ○ C. difficult and different

☆—☆—☆

The Race

The race was about to begin. The announcer asked for the crowd's attention. Then he told the runners to take their places at the starting line. For a **brief** moment, there was silence. Then the announcer yelled, "Ready! Set! Go!" The race was on. The runners were off around the track, and the crowd started cheering.

2. In this paragraph, the word **brief** must mean
   ○ A. rude
   ○ B. noisy
   ○ C. short

Practice Page 11

Name_____ Date_____

Read each paragraph. Then fill in the bubble that best completes each sentence.

The Eagle

The eagle is a powerful bird. It is also the national **symbol** of the United States. The bald eagle appears on different things that stand for our country. One of these is the Great Seal. You have probably seen the eagle in other places too. It is on U.S. dollar bills. It is also on U.S. coins such as quarters and half dollars.

1. In this paragraph, the word **symbol** must mean
   - ○ A. a picture that stands for something else
   - ○ B. a strong bird that flies around the country
   - ○ C. a kind of coin used in the United States

☆ ☆ ☆

A Good Plan

Jane's little brother wanted to see the fireworks. But it was hard for him to stay awake. Last year he fell asleep before they began. This year he was worried the same thing would happen. Jane had an idea. "Why don't you take a nap in the afternoon? Then you won't **doze** off so early tonight."

2. In this paragraph, the word **doze** must mean
   - ○ A. miss
   - ○ B. sleep
   - ○ C. worry

Name_____ Date_____

Read each paragraph. Then fill in the bubble
that best completes each sentence.

Rail Trails

What happens to unused railroad tracks?
In many parts of the U.S., people take
part in a Rails to Trails program. They
convert the tracks to trails. Smooth
paths are laid down where the tracks
once ran. People use these rail trails for
walking, jogging, skating, and bike
riding. In winter the trails are great for
cross-country skiing too.

1. In this paragraph, the word
   convert must mean
   ○ A. carry
   ○ B. discuss
   ○ C. change

A Fresh Flower

Don's class was learning about plants.
The teacher asked the students to
bring in a flower. Don chose a pretty
flower from his mother's garden. "How
will I get this to school?" he asked. "The
flower will **wilt** on the bus." Don's mother
showed him what to. She wrapped a wet
paper towel around the flower stem. "This
will keep your flower alive until you can
put it in water," she said.

2. In this paragraph, the
   word **wilt** must mean
   ○ A. spill over
   ○ B. lose freshness
   ○ C. grow slowly

Practice Page 13

Name_____ Date_____

Read each paragraph. Then fill in the bubble
that best completes each sentence.

Animal Meals

Some animals eat plants. Among
the big plant-eaters are
elephants and giraffes. When you see
cows and horses in a field, they are
eating plants, too. But many animals
eat meat. How do meat-eaters get
food? Wild animals that eat meat must
be good hunters. Usually their **prey** is
a smaller or weaker animal.

1. In this paragraph, the word
   prey must mean
   ○ A. saying a small prayer
   ○ B. animal that is hunted
   ○ C. how wild animals eat

☆—☆—☆

The Snow House

After the snow stopped, Rosa
went out to build a snow
house. She worked at it all
afternoon. That night she told her
family all about it at dinner. The next
morning Rosa couldn't wait to go outside.
She was shocked. Her snow house was a big
mess. "Who would **ruin** my house?" Rosa
asked. "The sun," said her dad. "It got
warmer and the snow melted."

2. In this paragraph, the
   word **ruin** must mean
   ○ A. cause damage
   ○ B. steal away
   ○ C. run around in

Name_____ Date_____

Read each paragraph. Then fill in the bubble
that best completes each sentence.

Furniture of the Past

In early America most furniture was
made by hand. Many people had
only a few pieces in their homes. So
furniture such as chairs sometimes had
more than one **function**. For example, a
ladder-backed chair could be used for
sitting. It could also be used as a
ladder. A rocking chair also served as a
baby's cradle. Some chairs could be
used to hold up shelves.

1. In this paragraph, the word
   function must mean

   ○ A. cushion

   ○ B. future

   ○ C. use

The Sandwich

Mr. Greenberg made a sandwich for his
lunch. As he set it on the table, the
doorbell rang. When Mr. Greenberg came
back, his sandwich was gone. But Mr.
Greenberg knew what had happened. He
had seen his dog **seize** the sandwich and
run. Right now Old Pal was sitting on the
porch licking his lips.

2. In this paragraph, the
   word **seize** must mean

   ○ A. grab

   ○ B. sniff

   ○ C. leave

Practice Page **15**   Name_____   Date_____

Read each paragraph. Then fill in the bubble
that best completes each sentence.

An Old Custom

A "baker's dozen" is 13 instead of 12. The custom
goes back to the year 1266 in England. Bakers
were making small loaves of bread. People did not
get what they paid for. So laws were passed. The
laws said that bakers had to meet **standards** set
by the government.
To be sure that they
met these measures,
bakers gave people an
extra loaf when they
ordered a dozen.

1. In this paragraph, the word **standards** must mean

◯ A. special stamps for bread

◯ B. well-known measures

◯ C. extra pieces of bread

Garbage Day

The bags of garbage were lined up at
the curb. Down the street came
the truck. At each stop the men got
out and picked up the bags. One by
one they **heaved** the heavy bags into
the back of the truck. As the bags
dropped into the truck, they made
crashing, clunking sounds.

2. In this paragraph, the word
heaved must mean

◯ A. pulled

◯ B. lifted

◯ C. opened

Practice Page **16**

Name_____ Date_____

Read each paragraph. Then fill in the bubble
that best completes each sentence.

The Mighty Python

Meet the python. This mighty snake grows up to 23 feet long. When the python is hungry, it needs a big meal. A python might grab a wild pig or small deer for dinner. The snake wraps itself around the animal until it is dead. Then the python opens its mouth and its dinner **vanishes** in one large gulp. After that, a python may not need to eat again for a while.

1. In this paragraph, the word **vanishes** must mean
   ○ A. disappears
   ○ B. runs away
   ○ C. stretches

Good Morning, Jade

Jade was always in a hurry. She ran into the kitchen for breakfast. She drank her juice in no time. She quickly dumped cereal into a bowl. Then she rushed to grab the pitcher of milk. "Slow down, Jade," her mother said. But it was too late. The pitcher slipped. Milk **gushed** out onto Jade's cereal and over the table as well. Jade cleaned up the mess. "Did you see how fast that milk came out?" she said.

2. In this paragraph, the word **gushed** must mean
   ○ A. gasped
   ○ B. dripped
   ○ C. poured

Practice Page 17

Name_____ Date_____

Read each paragraph. Then fill in the bubble
that best completes each sentence.

Body Temperature

As you climb out of the swimming pool, a breeze blows up. You can't find your towel. You are chilly. You begin to shiver. What makes you shiver? When your body temperature drops, a part of your brain quickly **reacts**. It takes control of your muscles and makes you shiver. When you shiver, you make extra body heat. This helps you warm up.

1. In this paragraph, the word **reacts** must mean

   ◯ A. warms up

   ◯ B. shuts down

   ◯ C. acts in response

A Book Sale

The town was having a used-book sale to raise money. People were asked to **donate** books they no longer wanted. Money from the sale would help to fix up the town park. Cole planned to give three books that were too easy for him. At the sale he hoped to buy other books that he hadn't yet read.

2. In this paragraph, the word **donate** must mean

   ◯ A. read

   ◯ B. dump

   ◯ C. give

Name_____ Date_____

Read each paragraph. Then fill in the bubble
that best completes each sentence.

Henson's Medal

Matthew Henson was an explorer. He was one of the two men who first reached the North Pole. It was a big victory. The year was 1909. One explorer, Robert Peary, became famous. He was given many honors. But Henson, a black man, did not become well known until 1944. In that year he was given a medal for his **outstanding** service to the U.S. Today Henson is honored for his great deed.

1. In this paragraph, the word **outstanding** must mean
   - ○ A. outdoor
   - ○ B. really great
   - ○ C. long

Lunchtime

Mrs. Hill entered the crowded lunchroom. She went through the line and chose her food. When she paid, Mrs. Hill looked around for a place to sit. There were no empty tables. Mrs. Hill spotted a table where people were laughing and talking. They seemed to be having a good time. "That's a **merry** group," she thought. "I'll join them."

2. In this paragraph, the word **merry** must mean
   - ○ A. jolly
   - ○ B. hungry
   - ○ C. crowded

Practice Page 19

Name_____ Date_____

Read each paragraph. Then fill in the bubble
that best completes each sentence.

Air Highways

Big cities have lots of air traffic. So the air space over these cities is divided into airways. These are like highways for planes. Each airway has a number. The airways also have speed limits. How do pilots know where the airways are? Control towers **beam** radio signals to show the airways. Pilots follow the signals just as drivers use road signs.

1. In this paragraph, the word **beam** must mean
   ○ A. send
   ○ B. smile
   ○ C. speed

At the Cabin

The cabin had been closed up all winter. Inside, it was dim and **gloomy**. Spiderwebs hung in the corners. Dust covered the floors. Mia said, "Let's make this place more cheerful." She opened the wooden shutters to let in light. Then she began sweeping and dusting. Soon the cabin would be ready for summer fun.

2. In this paragraph, the word **gloomy** must mean
   ○ A. dark
   ○ B. clean
   ○ C. cheery

Name_____ Date_____

Read each paragraph. Then fill in the bubble
that best completes each sentence.

Animals Now Gone

Have you ever heard of a dodo? This bird once lived on an island in the Indian Ocean. But the dodo is **extinct**. It died out hundreds of years ago. Many other animals have become extinct too. One example is a kind of zebra called a quagga. Other examples are all the dinosaurs. Today people work to save animals that are in danger of dying out.

1. In this paragraph, the word **extinct** must mean
   ○ A. excused
   ○ B. striped
   ○ C. no longer alive

Garden Helper

Amber liked to help her dad work in the garden. Today he was watering the plants. Amber knew that Dad worried when there wasn't any rain. "It's hard to keep the soil **moist** in this heat," said Dad. "The plants will dry out if they don't get enough water."

2. In this paragraph, the word **moist** must mean
   ○ A. wet
   ○ B. rich
   ○ C. dry

Name_____ Date_____

Read each paragraph. Then fill in the bubble
that best completes each sentence.

Who Will It Be?

Do you ever think about the person you might
someday marry? Many years ago girls in England
followed this **custom**: They wrote the
names of different boys on slips of
paper. They rolled each paper inside
some clay. Then they dropped the
clay into water. They waited for the
first piece of paper to float to the
top. The name on that paper was a
girl's future sweetheart.

1. In this paragraph, the word
   custom must mean
   - ○ A. old art program
   - ○ B. way of doing things
   - ○ C. someone who shops

Setting the Table

It was Joe's **chore** to set the table for
supper. Each night he put out dishes
and silverware for four people. One day
Joe got a phone call. That night he set the
table for six people. His sister teased him.
"Can't you count?" she asked. But then the
doorbell rang. It was Grandma and
Grandpa. "Good job, Joe," said Mom.

2. In this paragraph, the
   word **chore** must mean
   - ○ A. choose
   - ○ B. job
   - ○ C. count

Practice Page 22

Name_____ Date_____

Read each paragraph. Then fill in the bubble that best completes each sentence.

A Cane Custom

Long ago most American men had canes or walking sticks. Sometimes women had them too. People didn't use canes because they were lame. The canes were really for fashion. They gave people a sense of style. A man felt more like a gentleman when he was out **strolling** with a fancy walking stick.

1. In this paragraph, the word **strolling** must mean
   - ○ A. walking
   - ○ B. stylish
   - ○ C. leaning

The Bike Ride

Sam and Peggy were riding their bikes. Suddenly, Sam stopped and pointed. Peggy looked. There in the field next to them were two deer. One was quite small. Peggy opened her mouth to say something, but Sam put a finger to his lips. Then a car came by. The loud noise **startled** the deer, and off they ran.

2. In this paragraph, the word **startled** must mean
   - ○ A. harmed
   - ○ B. struck
   - ○ C. surprised

Name_____ Date_____

Read each paragraph. Then fill in the bubble
that best completes each sentence.

London Bobbies

To the people of London, England, a bobby is a **familiar** sight. A bobby is a police officer. Why are these workers called bobbies? They are named for Sir Robert (Bobby) Peel. He formed the police force in London in 1829. At that time a lot of people in the city were breaking the law. Today bobbies still make sure the laws are followed in London.

1. In this paragraph, the word **familiar** must mean

○ A. well-known

○ B. in a family

○ C. strange

Where's Owen?

Emma looked up and down the street. There was no sign of Owen. He was so **seldom** late. Where could he be? Emma looked at her watch. For Owen to be 15 minutes late was really unusual. Then, suddenly, Owen appeared around the corner. His leg was in a cast. No wonder it took him so long to get to their meeting place!

2. In this paragraph, the word **seldom** must mean

○ A. rarely

○ B. often

○ C. misplaced

Name_____   **Date**_____

Read each paragraph. Then fill in the bubble
that best completes each sentence.

Cats and Dogs

Animals have different ways to
protect themselves. Suppose a
strange dog **threatens** a cat. What
does the cat do? It stretches its legs
and arches its back. It fluffs its fur
and turns so its side faces the dog.
All this makes the cat look much
bigger. In case the dog doesn't get
the idea, the cat also hisses!

1. In this paragraph, the word
threatens must mean

   ◯ A. causes a feeling of joy

   ◯ B. wants to make friends with

   ◯ C. shows signs of hurting

Hide and Seek

At Cole's party, the guests played a game
of hide-and-seek. It was Cole's turn
to hide. He planned to **crouch** behind a
large flowerpot on the porch. But when he
got there, his dog, Rags, was already
sleeping behind the pot. There was no time
to find another place. Quickly, Cole bent
down next to his dog. Rags began to bark,
and the guests soon found Cole.

2. In this paragraph, the
word **crouch** must mean

   ◯ A. crumble

   ◯ B. stoop

   ◯ C. sleep

Practice Page **25**

Name_____   Date_____

Read each paragraph. Then fill in the bubble that best completes each sentence.

Volcanoes

An active volcano is quite a sight. Very hot rock boils miles below the top of the volcano. The boiling rock gives off gases. Over time these gases rise to the top of the volcano. Then they blow holes called **vents** in the volcano. Soon great clouds of gas and dust pour from the vents and shoot high in the sky. Hot rock flows out of the vents and down the sides of the volcano.

1. In this paragraph, the word **vents** must mean

○ A. openings

○ B. winds

○ C. viewings

Aunt Polly's Wash

On Saturday morning Aunt Polly did a big load of wash. "It's such a fine day," she said. "I think I'll hang the clothes on the line outside. Then they will **flutter** in the wind and dry." So Aunt Polly hung up her clean clothes. Sure enough, they began to flap. This upset all the birds in the yard, but Aunt Polly was very happy.

2. In this paragraph, the word **flutter** must mean

○ A. blow away

○ B. wave fast

○ C. make noise

Practice Page 26

Name_____ Date_____

Read each paragraph. Then fill in the bubble
that best completes each sentence.

Good at Business

Madame C. J. Walker had her own business. She sold products for hair care. She also owned beauty shops in many U.S. cities. She set up schools to **train** people to work for her. By 1919 Madame Walker had made a lot of money. She became the first black female millionaire. She gave money to help many black groups. She also helped schools and needy people.

1. In this paragraph, the word **train** must mean
   ○ A. railroad
   ○ B. teach
   ○ C. save

Harry's Show

Harry was telling his family about a show with a juggler. "He wore funny clothes," said Harry. "And he had lots of balls. He could keep them all in the air at the same time." Harry's father was puzzled. How had Harry seen a show? Their TV was broken. "Where did this show **occur**?" Dad asked. "Did you see it at preschool?" Harry shook his head. "It happened in a book!" he said.

2. In this paragraph, the word **occur** must mean
   ○ A. toss around
   ○ B. turn off
   ○ C. take place

Name_____ Date_____

Read each paragraph. Then fill in the bubble
that best completes each sentence.

The Flamingo

The flamingo is a bird with long legs and a long neck.
It takes its food from the lakes where it lives. How
does a flamingo **obtain** its food? It lowers its beak upside
down into the water. Then it sweeps its
head back and forth with its
beak open. In this way it
catches its favorite
food—shrimp.

1. In this paragraph, the
   word **obtain** must mean
   ○ A. cook
   ○ B. chew
   ○ C. get

Stan's Picture

Stan was drawing a picture. It showed
his sister's wedding. She had worn a
long white dress. Her husband wore a
black tuxedo. Stan put them both in the
picture. "You forgot my flowers," said his
sister. Stan thought for a moment. "What
color were they?" His sister answered,
"They were the **hue** of an evening sky."

2. In this paragraph, the
   word **hue** must mean
   ○ A. stars
   ○ B. shape
   ○ C. color

Practice Page 28

Name_____ Date_____

Read each paragraph. Then fill in the bubble
that best completes each sentence.

A Food Story

Long ago there were no freezers or tin cans. People had to think of ways to keep food from going bad. They used different ways to **preserve** food. For example, they dried some fruits, vegetables, and meat. Another way to keep fruits was to make jams from them. People also used salt and water to make food last longer. Some foods such as potatoes could be stored in a cold place.

1. In this paragraph, the word **preserve** must mean
   ○ A. spoil or destroy
   ○ B. buy or grow
   ○ C. keep or save

Sick in Bed

When Terry was sick, she had to stay in bed for a few days. Terry didn't mind. She found lots of ways to **amuse** herself. Her favorite way of spending time was reading. She also did a lot of drawing. In the evenings Terry had fun playing board games with her sister. Once in a while they even watched TV.

2. In this paragraph, the word **amuse** must mean
   ○ A. entertain
   ○ B. annoy
   ○ C. recover

Reading Passages That Build Comprehension: Context Clues Scholastic Teaching Resources

Practice Page **29**

Name_____ Date_____

Read each paragraph. Then fill in the bubble
that best completes each sentence.

An Amazing Plant

Can a plant grow through ice? At least one
plant can. The blue moonwort grows on the
mountains in Switzerland. These mountains
are covered with snow and ice during the
winter. Early each spring the moonwort
soaks up some of the melting snow through
its roots. Then its stem starts pushing up.
Soon the plant **bores** a hole right through
the ice! Then it begins to bloom.

2. In this paragraph, the
word **bores** must mean

○ A. tires

○ B. drills

○ C. grows

A Good Cookie

An ant spotted something on the step.
It looked like a cookie. Quickly, the
ant raced back to its nest to let others know.
Soon a line of ants made its way to the
cookie. But just then a large foot appeared.
It stepped on the cookie and **crushed** it. The
ants didn't mind. They waited until the foot
moved. Then they picked up the small
pieces and carried them to the nest.

2. In this paragraph, the
word **crush** must mean

○ A. break into pieces

○ B. made a noise

○ C. carried away

Practice Page **30** Name_____ Date_____

Read each paragraph. Then fill in the bubble that best completes each sentence.

The Button Story

Why are there buttons on the sleeves of men's jackets? Some say it is because of Frederick the Great. This king led his men in many wars. He liked the troops to look neat. But their sleeves were always dirty. That's because the soldiers wiped the sweat from their faces on their sleeves. Frederick was **outraged** about this. He was so angry he had buttons put on the uniform sleeves of all his men. It's hard to wipe your face on a button.

1. In this paragraph, the word **outraged** must mean
   ○ A. angry
   ○ B. sweaty
   ○ C. pleased

☆ ☆ ☆

Ice Cream, Please

Connor worked in an ice cream shop. On a summer day he was very busy. It seemed that everyone loved ice cream then. Each morning Connor checked his supplies. Most people ordered cones. The flavors they chose would **vary** though. Connor was careful to have plenty of each flavor on hand.

2. In this paragraph, the word **vary** must mean
   ○ A. plenty
   ○ B. differ
   ○ C. taste

Practice Page 31

Name_____ Date_____

Read each paragraph. Then fill in the bubble
that best completes each sentence.

The Earth and Sun

In 1632 people thought that the sun
moved around Earth. They didn't
think Earth moved at all. That year
Galileo wrote a book. He said that
Earth moved around the sun. People
were upset. Galileo was told he would
be killed unless he said his book was a
lie. So Galileo said he had written a lie.
But he knew that didn't **alter** the truth.
For Earth does move around the sun.

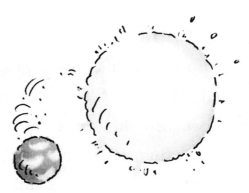

1. In this paragraph, the
word **alter** must mean

○ A. worship

○ B. renew

○ C. change

Vito's Test

Vito did **poorly** on a test in school.
This upset him because he had
worked hard. Vito's dad had an idea. He
took Vito to see an eye doctor. Sure enough,
Vito needed glasses. Now Vito can see
better, and he does well on his tests too.

2. In this paragraph, the
word **poorly** must mean

○ A. not well

○ B. just okay

○ C. slowly

Name_____   Date_____

Read each paragraph. Then fill in the bubble
that best completes each sentence.

The Octopus

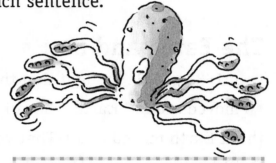

Most people think an octopus swims with its arms. After all, it has eight of them. But an octopus uses its arms for crawling, not swimming. To swim, an octopus draws water into its body. Then it **squirts** the water out through a tube under its head. The force of the water spraying out moves the octopus backward through the sea.

1. In this paragraph, the word **squirts** must mean
   ○ A. sucks
   ○ B. sprays
   ○ C. dribbles

Hungry on a Hike

The hikers hoped to get to the top of the mountain by lunchtime. Selma was hungry. She thought they would never get there. Finally, the group leader stopped and pointed. "Do you see the rocks that **jut** out up there?" he asked. "That is where we are going." Selma saw rocks that leaned out from the mountainside. She began to walk faster. She couldn't wait for her turkey sandwich.

2. In this paragraph, the word **jut** must mean
   ○ A. grow up
   ○ B. move around
   ○ C. stick out

Name_____ Date_____

Read each paragraph. Then fill in the bubble
that best completes each sentence.

Stone Stories

Some people think that certain stones bring good luck. Other people believe that special stones **prevent** different problems. For example, diamonds are thought to keep away nightmares. Garnets are supposed to keep people free from injury. Pearls and jade are thought to keep wearers from harm.

1. In this paragraph, the word **prevent** must mean
   ○ A. to keep from happening
   ○ B. to cause trouble
   ○ C. to make believe

Randy's Art

Randy spent a lot of time drawing. Her teacher, Miss Begay, looked at Randy's pictures. They were good. Randy had a real **flair**. "Why don't you enter some pictures in the school art show?" Miss Begay said. At first Randy wasn't sure, but finally she entered three pictures. Best of all, one of her pictures won a prize.

2. In this paragraph, the word **flair** must mean
   ○ A. talent
   ○ B. flame
   ○ C. prize

Name_____ Date_____

Read each paragraph. Then fill in the bubble that best completes each sentence.

Fishy Names

Some fish names come from the Latin language. One example is the trout. Its name comes from the Latin word *trocta*. This means "greedy fish." Fishermen will tell you that this is true. Trout do have this **trait**. They are big eaters and go after any bait that moves. Salmon are known for leaping out of the water. Their name comes from the Latin word *salmon*, which means "leaping fish."

1. In this paragraph, the word **trait** must mean

○ A. feature

○ B. tail

○ C. problem

A Book for Grandfather

Hector carefully arranged the photos on the page. Under each photo Hector wrote a sentence. He told who was in the picture or where it was taken. Hector was going to give the book to Grandfather on his birthday. It would help him **recall** a lot of family events. Grandfather liked to talk about past times.

2. In this paragraph, the word **recall** must mean

○ A. remove

○ B. reform

○ C. remember

Name_____ Date_____

Read each paragraph. Then fill in the bubble
that best completes each sentence.

All About Trees

Suppose you are lost in a forest. You might find your way by looking at the trees. **Observe** them carefully. The side of a tree with the most leaves and branches is the south side. The tops of trees lean toward the south too. If you study the bark closely, you'll see that it is lighter and brighter on one side. That is also the south side. But if you see moss at the base of a tree, it will be on the north side.

1. In this paragraph, the word **observe** must mean

   ○ A. circle

   ○ B. ignore

   ○ C. examine

New Rollerblades

The first time that Clay tried out his rollerblades, he learned an important lesson. Parts of the sidewalk were not very good for skating. In these places the sidewalk was bumpy and **uneven**. Clay found that it was much easier to keep his balance on smooth sections.

2. In this paragraph, the word **uneven** must mean

   ○ A. unfair

   ○ B. not straight

   ○ C. not level

Name_____ Date_____

Read each paragraph. Then fill in the bubble that best completes each sentence. Underline a clue that helped you.

Writing About Pippi

Sometimes writers have trouble getting started. They **stall** for time. For example, Astrid Lindgren couldn't make herself write about Pippi Longstocking for a long time. Then she hurt her ankle and had to stay at home. Lindgren couldn't put off her work anymore. She began her book.

1. In this paragraph, the word **stall** must mean
○ A. trade
○ B. start
○ C. delay

Honey at Home

Cara's cat didn't like to be left alone. Cara never knew what Honey would do when the family was out. Sometimes the cat just slept. But sometimes she was bad. One day Cara found a big mess in the bathroom. Honey had unrolled the toilet paper. It was in **shreds**. Bits of it were everywhere. It took a long time to clean up Honey's mess.

2. In this paragraph, the word **shreds** must mean
○ A. rolls
○ B. pieces
○ C. squares

Assessment 2 Name_____ Date_____

Read each paragraph. Then fill in the bubble that best completes each sentence. Underline a clue that helped you.

What Happened?

Why did dinosaurs disappear? Scientists have different ideas. One possible idea is that there was a long **drought** during the time of dinosaurs. This dry period caused changes in the plants that grew on Earth. These changes meant that the dinosaurs didn't have enough sources of food to live.

1. In this paragraph, the word **drought** must mean
   ○ A. stormy season
   ○ B. period without rain
   ○ C. cloud of dust

The Town Parade

Each year there was a parade in Marco's town. The night before, people blew up huge balloons. They decorated floats. The bands practiced their music. Marco wanted to see all this activity. His mother said he should wait and see the parade. Marco began to **plead**. He asked his mother over and over until she said yes.

2. In this paragraph, the word **plead** must mean
   ○ A. beg
   ○ B. praise
   ○ C. march

Assessment 3

Name_____ Date_____

Read each paragraph. Then fill in the bubble that best completes each sentence. Underline a clue that helped you.

Dr. Blackwell

Elizabeth Blackwell was the first woman doctor in the United States. She became a doctor in 1849. At that time no hospital would hire a woman in this role. So Elizabeth Blackwell started her own hospital. As a doctor, she had a big **concern**. She was interested in helping people to live in healthier conditions. Dr. Blackwell worked hard to help make this happen.

1. In this paragraph, the word **concern** must mean
   ○ A. care or interest
   ○ B. kind of work
   ○ C. large office

Bad Idea

The campers thought it would be fun to play a **prank** on their counselor. They decided to put salt in his toothpaste. However, Bud did not think this joke was funny. He made the campers use the salty toothpaste every night for a week.

2. In this paragraph, the word **prank** must mean
   ○ A. game
   ○ B. trick
   ○ C. flavor

Student Record Sheet

Name _____ Date _____

Date	Practice Page # _____	Number Correct	Comments

Answers

☆ ☆ ☆

Page 5:
1. sun
2. The most important part of this system is the sun.
3. The solar system could be called the "sun system."
4. looking in the dictionary

Page 8:
1. B
2. A
3. C

Page 9:
1. B
2. A

Page 10:
1. C
2. B

Page 11:
1. A
2. C

Page 12:
1. C
2. C

Page 13:
1. A
2. B

Page 14:
1. C
2. B

Page 15:
1. B
2. B

Page 16:
1. C
2. A

Page 17:
1. A
2. A

Page 18:
1. B
2. C

Page 19:
1. A
2. B

Page 20:
1. C
2. B

Page 21:
1. B
2. A

Page 22:
1. C
2. A

Page 23:
1. B
2. B

Page 24:
1. A
2. C

Page 25:
1. C
2. C

Page 26:
1. B
2. A

Page 27:
1. A
2. A

Page 28:
1. C
2. A

Page 29:
1. B
2. B

Page 30:
1. A
2. C

Page 31:
1. A
2. A

Page 32:
1. C
2. B

Page 33:
1. A
2. B

Page 34:
1. B
2. C

Page 35:
1. C
2. C

Page 36:
1. C
2. A

Page 37:
1. B
2. A

Page 38:
1. A
2. B

Page 39:
1. C
2. A

Page 40:
1. B
2. C

Page 41:
1. A
2. A

Page 42:
1. A
2. C

Page 43:
1. C
2. C

Page 44:
1. C; put off her work
2. B; bits

Page 45:
1. B; dry period
2. A; asked his mother over and over

Page 46:
1. A; She was interested in helping people
2. B; this joke